To Ajay

I'll Have a
Martini, Please!

Thanks for th
coming to Sip & Chat
with me!

Tamara N. Harvey

Tamara N. Harvey
Mar 17 2019

For All the Moms who need more #MeTime & a
Martini!

"I like to have a martini,
two at the very most.
After three I'm under the table,
after four I'm under the host."

~Dorothy Parker~

Contents

Introduction

When I started writing this book, I was taking a break from writing my first mystery novel. I was stumped and felt like the characters had stopped talking to me. So, I took a break to reflect and gather my thoughts. I began to journal. After the first few days, I decided to continue until the end of the month to record the next thirty days of my life. I have documented these days, unscripted, just me sharing when I could remember, and keeping it as real as can be. That's right, just me living, loving, and laughing. Moreover, as a bonus, I'll share random things that cross my mind, things that I #hashtag, and poetry that I wrote. Feel free to start in whichever part you like.

First, let me explain to you how I came up with the title of this book. I mentioned that I am including random things that I #hashtag well, when I am going through most of those things, I end up feeling like I want and should have a martini! "Why a martini?" It's my favorite drink. It's a sexy drink served in an appealing glass. I love them! Ketel One martini to be specific! For those of you who don't know what a martini is, here you go. The perfect martini is quite simple. The ingredients include three parts: three olives and vodka! Merely pour vodka into a shaker filled with ice and shake vigorously. Strain into a chilled martini glass. Garnish with three olives.

That's all fine and dandy if you're looking for a "perfect martini," but I'm not! First, I don't care for olives. Second, there are just too many great-tasting juices and liqueurs to add for extra flavor. My favorite mixes are cranberry, orange, and sometimes even apple juice. Alternatively, I'll buy some CIROC (flavored vodka).

At this very moment, it's about 3:30 in the afternoon and 25 degrees outside. The twins and I have been home all week enjoying our days off during winter break. We haven't done much of anything. Most days the twins don't even want to get dressed, and the weather makes me not want to go out. Like I need a manicure and pedicure, but the way my arthritis has set up, it's too goddamn cold. My bones are aching, and my knees are inflamed, ugh! "I'll have a martini, please!"

PART I

30 DAYS OF MY LIFE

Last Friday of 2017

That's right, today is *Friday, December 29, 2017,* and the #lastFridayof2017 and one of the Trending Topics on Twitter this morning. And my tweet for that topic was for everyone to order my book *I Love Hate My Hair (My Journey with Alopecia)* available in paperback or eBook from Amazon, Barnes and Noble, Google Play, Apple iBook, or Kobo books! There, got that plug in!

For some reason, I woke up in the middle of the night with a toothache, and I had to pee. Yup, I have a weak bladder since the twins, plus I drank hot tea before bed. I prayed a special prayer for healing because I felt like maybe somebody had made a voodoo doll with my face on it. Like WTF, is this my season for aches and pains? I mean, this month I have felt like I am either aching or hurting everywhere—got me channeling my inner @khiathugmisses in here singing, "Everything hurts, my neck, my back, my knees and that's a fact!"

LOL—#sorrynotsorry. I hope you're ready because I will have you laughing with me!

Anyway, I got up early to see my husband off to work, and I fixed him a cheese egg on a bagel to go with his morning cup of coffee. I love coffee too, but not more than my martini. After he left, I grabbed my cup and hopped back upstairs. Yes, I'm literally hopping because my knee is busted—fluid, inflammation, meniscus tears. Goddamnit! I climbed back into bed and picked up my latest read: *The Subtle Art of Not Giving a Fuck* (TSAON-GAF). I am so enjoying this book right now.

The twins woke up about mid-morning and I knew "my time" was up. Hopped back downstairs and made them some oatmeal along with a cup of orange juice. Then it was back upstairs to make some phone calls, schedule some appointments, and so on. I Facetimed my husband a few times, just to fuck with him, and I had my usual morning talk with my mother.

But afterward, out of nowhere, I had this moment of weakness and began to have a pity party. Not about anything, but just the fact that everything seemed to be going to the left for some reason. And I kept wondering, *Why?* Now, if you're anything like me, you read your horoscope every day and take "something" from it! I'm a Scorpio and proud of it. And I have T-shirts and a tattoo to prove it.

Today's Instagram scope, from @ScorpioMystique starts off by saying "Not everyone's always going to understand your vision, Scorpio." And I was like, "Say no more, Fam." It goes on to say we should focus on our ideas, etc. Then finally, she ends with "Keep creating." And create I will. My birthday is November 11, and my goal for 2017 was to finish my book titled, *Scorpio Scorned* and send it to the publisher by the end of the year, so it would be published by summer 2018. It's a murder mystery, and I swear the characters just stopped talking to me. So, I decided to keep working on this one and come back to it when I can be more creative! There, it's done.

Well, I've got to break for a bit and track my pizza from Papa John's. The pizza arrived within the fifty-five to sixty-five minutes, and we were all glad it did. Half cheese/pepperoni pan pizza is our favorite, along with plain wings and cheese sticks. Oh, and for a treat a two-liter of Pepsi.

Since the twins were determined to do nothing but play their new PS4 and Nintendo DS or whatever games, I decided to #binge-watch movies, wash a load or two, and clean up in between. I usually work from home two days a week and go to the office the other three. But since I was off this entire week, I wasn't sure how to act. But what I did know was that I wanted to do what I wanted.

After we ate, I showered and began to remove my hair unit. I was having a moment, a meltdown, or whatever you want to call it. After it was off, I cleaned my scalp good with alcohol and then oil. Next, I sat down and moisturized my hair with my favorite Mane and Tale Revitalizing Creme. Then parted and braided it. When all else fails with my hair, I always resort back to my girl-friends a.k.a. wigs!

Later in the afternoon, I called my husband to check what time he would be getting off work and asked him to bring me something to drink home please! Either grab some martini mix or my favorite wine. Unfortunately, the Wine & Spirits store (Why do they call it that?) was all out of both. Go figure. So, he had to grab my third option, Angry Orchard (Crisp Apple).

By now, it's after 8:00 p.m., and I'm finished watching movies and gearing up for my favorite Friday night shows—*48 Hours* and *20/20*. Most of the time I'm watching the latter in bed, and relaxed. I end up falling asleep missing the end! But not tonight, baby, I'm watching in the living room with the lights on determined to help solve this case. I cracked open that Angry Orchard, and about ten minutes into the episode, my daughter came down for a drink and ended up spilling half the gallon of milk EVERYWHERE! Yes, I'm yelling!

This is what happens when she continues to try to do things on her own, instead of asking for help. And I'm not happy. Now I must get up out of the recliner and go into the kitchen to help her clean up this mess. Damnit…I can't bend down because of my knee, and I just ended up grabbing the mop and getting it up. I fixed her chocolate milk and sent her upstairs. "Just leave me alone!" I'm starting to feel like I need a B-R-E-A-K!!!

Saturday Love

*S*aturday, December 30, 2017. "Never on Sunday, Monday's too soon, Tuesday and Wednesday just won't do. Thursday and Friday the weekend begins, but our Saturday Love WILL NEVER END. Sugar!" In my best Cherrelle voice baby… I'm in a good mood this morning despite the bitter cold temperature, and the fact that my husband gets up before the sun to go to work. I'm glad I work for the government and have the weekends off.

As soon as he left, back upstairs I went with my favorite Emoji coffee mug to catch a few minutes of the depressing news and then a quick FREE movie on demand before the twins woke up. I was in luck this morning and able to get in two movies, because the twins didn't wake up until after 11:00 a.m. First up was *Bernard and Doris*. Susan Sarandon looked terrific as a blonde, and I loved the plot twists of the movie. I had to go downstairs for another cup of coffee by this time I had watched *Silver*

Linings Playbook. I had to rewind some of it because the twins wanted to see what I was laughing out loud so much for. I mean I cried a few times throughout, but at the end when they danced and that final letter and kiss! Damnit, I didn't want to cry, but the tears started to flow.

The twins managed to fix their own bowls of cereal for breakfast this morning. Yay! I knew they could do it. Honestly, sometimes I believe they think they're making me feel important by asking me to do EVERYTHING for them. Who said the #MomLife would be easy? Nobody. I called my mom for our daily talk, and she was still in bed herself. I told her that I was aching so bad and that I didn't really feel like getting up either. She immediately blamed it on the freezing weather. Now, I'm not about to debate the family on certain superstitions, etc., but I refuse to believe that each/every time it rains, from this day forward, that I'm going to have aches and pain because of my arthritis. There must be another way.

I was already addicted to Facebook, Twitter, and Instagram, but let me tell you, now the Snap Chat filters and the awesome information on Pinterest are giving them a run for their money. I was on Pinterest last night for about an hour looking up natural herbs and/or remedies for my arthritis. As soon as I get out of here, I'm taking a trip to the Giant or Trader Joe's to find some of these. I'm also thinking about acupuncture in addition to or in placement of physical therapy that I know Ortho Maryland is going to suggest I have for my knee.

One thing that I used to religiously do on Saturday was visit the hair salon and nail shop. But those days are over, or at least on a regular basis. My daughter would go with me or separately. But since she's suddenly become a cry baby, I've been struggling to do her hair myself. We started about 1:30 p.m., and by the time we took a break here and there for lunch and to stretch, it was about 4:00 p.m. when I was finished taking out her beads and plaits. She performed so much that #ICant finish tonight. First thing tomorrow morning we're shampooing/conditioning/styling—but pigtails this time. And I WILL BE GOING TO GET A MANI/PEDI. I don't care if it's 18 degrees.

Now that they're out of my hair, or my room, I'm going to dive back into TSAONGAF! Until tomorrow... Happy #NewYearsEveEve—Can you believe that was also a trending topic on Twitter?

Pamper Me Please!

*S*unday, December 31, 2017. It's New Year's Eve and I am so excited. The first thing that was on my mind was getting up and going to the nail salon for a manicure and pedicure. I received a gift certificate from the family, so I was not going to waste any time. But first, I had to make my way downstairs to turn off the Christmas lights outside and put on a fresh pot of coffee.

Within minutes everyone else was up. After I enjoyed my cup of joe, I showered and got dressed. Before I left I cooked breakfast for the family and broke camp. By the time I arrived at the nail salon it was 1:30 p.m. and everybody and their sister must have had the same idea. The wait wasn't long, but I ended up spending two hours in there. Ugh…I called home to check in on the family and they were chilling. So, I decided to go to the grocery store and Dollar General. These were not my favorite places, but necessary weekly!

Almost an hour later, I called home to let them know I was making my way back and would need help with the bags. All the walking, and sitting during the pedicure, made my knees so stiff, and I suppose the freezing cold temperatures may have played a role in the way I felt as well. I rubbed down with Salonpas before I left, but I desperately needed to ice these knees when I got settled.

Once we put the food away, I got busy cooking. First, I broiled two steaks and made some French fries for the twins. Then the lasagna. And last but certainly not least collard greens and black-eyed peas. Why do we need to eat them again? If it's for good luck, then I need to eat the entire one-pound bag—and for dessert WEIS Bakery "New Year" cupcakes and vanilla bean ice cream. Yummy...and everyone else in the Harvey household agreed.

By the time I sat down to write this entry, it was about 11:15 p.m. I managed to get all that done and wash MY dirty clothes. That's another thing that we are "supposed" to do before we bring in the new year. I don't know who made these up, but I follow them religiously.

The Ravens lost against the Bengals tonight, so we're out of the playoffs. That was a real bummer because we only lost by 4 points. Nevertheless, I will bring in the new year with my Ravens gear on (purple toes included) and my "HAPPY NEW YEAR" headband and party favors courtesy of Walmart. Until tomorrow, friends!

Happy New Year!

We managed to stay up and bring in the New Year wearing headbands and blowing our horns! We also watched some fireworks outside in the neighborhood. Our local news channel hosted a nice show with community talent and fireworks as well; however, I had to tune in to Ryan Seacrest to watch Mariah Carey and Britney Spears. Mariah looked great but was mad they didn't have her tea! LOL…I love her! By 12:30 a.m. I was walking the twins upstairs and getting ready for bed. I was completely wiped out.

January 1, 2018. My alarm went off at 6:45 a.m. like it does every Monday morning, but I just hit Stop and rolled back over. Then I was awoken by the wretched sound of the Maury Povich show. There was a time when I watched it and laughed, but now it's just a Hot M-E-S-S! My husband was watching it and it was totally annoying. I hopped up, grabbed the cane, and headed right downstairs for the coffee pot! Ugh…

By the time I got back upstairs to brush my teeth and wash my face, that dreadful visitor greeted me: "Aunt Dot" PMS…Why do we still have a menstrual cycle at age forty-eight? Why? Like "Happy New Year Bih!" (in my Plies voice). I love him too! I know I shouldn't let it, but this time of the month is bad for me. I just get into a funk, and I know it, and I stay there for a period. I shut down and just let the day play out.

I knew first on my plate was to get baby girl's hair done. Washing her hair is quite the task, and she doesn't want to do it. I had decided I wasn't going to make breakfast this morning because when I came back from shopping yesterday, everyone had left their plates and cups from yesterday's breakfast on the table. And that, my friends, is a faux pas for Mommy! There. Call me Petty Patty or Whatever the Fuck, but there will be no breakfast cooked today! Not by me.

My son and I cleaned up the basement and I washed a load or two. By noon I made my way back upstairs to get the hair thing going. That took us about three hours! Yes, that's right. The only thing left to do after that ordeal was to make slime. And make slime we did! Glow in the dark, scented, and with glitter! I'm giving everyone an hour or two to themselves before dinner. Then it's back to our regularly scheduled program. I am so glad that they are going back to school tomorrow and get around their friends and away from these video games, and I can work from home alone!

Ortho Maryland

Tuesday, January 2, 2018. I had a follow-up appointment at Ortho Maryland today to discuss the MRI I had on December 27. So, it turns out that I have tears in my meniscus in my left knee. Arthritis in front and back of my knee cap is visible as well, along with inflammation. Gee whiz…

Because it was right after the holiday, I didn't see my regular doctor, but the one on call, one who was stuck with being there the day after New Year's. After my consultation with him, I left there knowing I had to make the decision whether to have surgery or not. After all, I didn't want to continue taking the anti-inflammatory medication and hopping along.

Once I returned to work, I figured out when would be a good time for me to be on leave, then I called Ortho Maryland to schedule.

I scheduled my arthroscopy for *February 21, 2018*, and I pray that it goes well and gives me relief for this knee pain.

Happy Birthday, Junie

W *ednesday, January 3, 2018.* Today would have been my father's 66th birthday! I came downstairs to make morning coffee as usual, wished him a happy birthday, and lit the candle that I keep next to his urn and picture. Wow, sometimes I still can't believe it's been four years since he passed. Gone too soon!

Enjoy each moment you can with your parents, especially if they are sick and in a nursing home. I wish I would have spent more time with my dad when he had fallen sick, but to tell you the truth sometimes it was hard to see him like that. Nevertheless, I am glad that my kids and I got to see him when we did, and especially before he passed away.

CCBC

*F*riday, January 5, 2018. All I can say is Thank Goodness it's Friday! Before I go into the office today, I am heading to the Community College of Baltimore County to apply for graduation. That's right, after sixteen years of attending this community college off/on, I am FINALLY going to graduate. Or so I thought…

After spending $75 for the graduation fee and $12 to have my official transcript sent to a local university, CCBC notified me that I still had one course to complete. Turns out that because my last hiatus was more than two years, the course catalog changed, and I had to take one more "required" course.

I couldn't believe it! It was bad enough that I had quit and went back so many times, but to think that this semester wasn't the end of the road was a bummer. I sat back and thought, *Hell, I could've been a doctor as long it has taken me.* But you know what? The bottom line and the most important thing is that I am finishing, and I will graduate. I registered for my last course and look forward to receiving my Associate of Arts Degree in Human Services Counseling in June 2018! And after that, I'm headed to Stevenson University in hopes of finishing my bachelor's degree by the time my twins graduate from middle school. Be sure to check my social media for a selfie in my cap and gown.

Love Jones

Monday, *January 8, 2018.* My love jones is down. No, they are practically *underground.* Ladies, have you had any lip-locking, hip-thrusting, leg-bending, or wig-pulling sex lately? Neither have I, but I wouldn't mind. It's a little bit harder to have wild nights when you have kids. We don't usually close or lock our bedroom door, but I'm thinking we may need to consider doing so. Our kids are so used to just walking in our room to talk to us or climbing into bed with us when they can't sleep. I dread the night, or day, if they ever walk in on us when we're making out. Oh well, no worries about that this week.

Before I forget, I want to tell you all that I downloaded a terrific book today titled, *The Wake-Up Call* by Ash Cash. Order it 1) to support another black author, 2) to gain some knowledge about financial inspiration learned from 4:44, and 3) to take his Declaration of Financial Independence. Lord knows I needed this, and

I'm striving to increase my credit score and KEEP it up!

My absolute favorite app for taking pictures is Aristo. I think I will snap a selfie and post one before I log off Instagram tonight. A Selfie a Day Keeps the _____ away. [That blank can be filled in with several different words.]

Who cares what anyone else says? #LoveYourSelfie

Coffee in the Morning

*T*hursday, January 11, 2018. I'm up earlier than usual because my husband left for work earlier. See, I've never been an "early bird" and I don't think I'll ever be. Since I was up I made my way downstairs for my morning cup of coffee. I love to get my coffee within the first five to ten minutes after it's been brewed. Our personal preference for coffee is Maxwell House. Although, last year on vacation I was introduced to Folgers Black Silk and every now and again I must have it!

After I get my coffee, I come back upstairs and reach for my favorite book by Toni Sorter, *Prayers and Promises for Women*. And I skim through the contents to find what reading is suitable for how I'm feeling this morning. Today it was **Loneliness**. Now, I've had this book for years, but I don't recall this reading like I do some of the others. Which leads me to believe that I haven't felt this way in a long time.

The passage is from **Psalm 102:7**: *I watch and am as a sparrow alone upon the housetop.*

Some days I feel just like that lonely sparrow, Lord. Everyone else is crowded around the bird feeder, caring for their babies, or flitting to and for on urgent business, but I sit alone just watching. What am I looking for? Will I ever find a flock of my own to join? Will anyone ever fly up and join me on the housetop, easing this sense of separation I feel so acutely? Yet You tell me that not one sparrow falls without Your noticing and that I am of more value than many sparrows (**Matthew 10:29–31**). You see me there alone on my rooftop, Lord. You feel my loneliness, and suddenly I belong—and I can sing a song of joy. (Sorter 2003)

I prayed after that and finished my cup of coffee, because I only had about fifteen more minutes of "me time" before the kids woke up, and we had to get ready for school.

Cancer-Free

Today my mother received her results from her follow-up colonoscopy, and she is #cancer free. Praise God! Hallelujah! and any other positive praises you can think of. I am so happy for her and relieved. Watching her lose weight and not knowing why, then finding out she had cancer, and then watching her go through chemotherapy was a lot for her and all of us. With that in mind, I know that I must have a screening before the age of fifty, and I am not looking forward to it. It's like I know I must, but I don't want to think about another "possibility" of anything bad happening. Nothing.

You can bet your last dollar that as soon as possible she and I are going to Bonefish Grill for a nice cold martini! That's right, for good news there's always a reason for a delicious drink. We talk in the morning and share cup of coffee almost daily, but rarely do we have a "ladies" night and girl talk over a cocktail and bang-bang shrimp. We're overdue!

Chunky Monkey

I t's *Friday, January 12, 2018,* and tonight it's as cold as a
"witch's tit" (Is that even true?) outside! The kids and
I drove through the McDonald's drive-thru for din-
ner, and now I'm upstairs in my room with my new best
friend, Netflix. When all else fails, you eat a pint of Ben &
Jerry's. My favorite is Chunky Monkey. Banana ice cream
with fudge chunks and walnuts. NOTHING, and I mean
nothing, makes me feel better. I know that might sound
strange, but it's true. Let me tell you how you should eat a
pint of Ben & Jerry's. Grab yourself a *tablespoon* and crack
open that pint and dig in! Believe me, once you take that
first spoonful you won't want to stop.

I've gotten so crazy with the Chunky Monkey that
now I just pull up at 7-11, run straight back to the freez-
er, grab a pint, throw it up on the counter (with exact
change), and run back out! I don't even need a bag. This
week they have the nerve to have two pints on sale for
$9. Now, I know you're probably thinking, *That's not a*

sale, girlfriend. After the day I've had, I don't even care. I don't usually share my favorite ice cream either, but *sometimes* I will give a scoop or two to my son or husband (my daughter doesn't care for it). But here lately, they've been trying different Ben & Jerry's flavors to find their favorite. Good!

According to the BMI chart, I am obese! When I first saw that, I was scared and disappointed in myself. Like, how in the world did you let yourself get this heavy, Tammy? How? And then I looked down into the pint of my ice cream and thought, *Well, maybe this has a little something to do with it*. But then I caught myself and was like, "Nope." I know that Ben & Jerry's also makes sorbet, which has less calories. Who cares? It's Chunky Monkey that I want, and that's what I'll buy and eat.

Saturday, January 13, 2018. All I have to say is that there are sixty-five more days until spring! And I am looking forward to a break from these frigid temperatures. My little bones are aching and I'm exhausted.

But before I go to bed, I must log back into Facebook. I recall seeing a notification about memories on this date, and well, I need to see what I posted umm… three or four years ago on this date. Also, I want to make sure I didn't forget to wish any of my friends a happy birthday. Do you all find yourselves depending on Facebook for these too?

Call Me Carla

Monday, *January 15, 2018.* Because I put myself in a funk about my damn weight the last few days, I had to run out and buy something that would make me feel better.

If you guessed a new pair of shoes, you're wrong. It's not a purse either. I drove to Beauty 4 U, my favorite beauty store, yesterday and picked up a new wig; her name is Carla and she's platinum blonde and styled in a cute little bob. I'm happy too! I couldn't wait to update my profile picture with my cute, fresh style.

I know African American women aren't born with blonde hair, but this one has more fun when I'm wearing it. I also noticed that I get more compliments, likes, and comments with this look. That's interesting. But I'm not going to get into that, not right now.

Promise Myself

I got up early this morning, and right after my sip of Nestle lemon-flavored water (I love their flavored water), I made my way downstairs to make my cup of coffee. When I came back upstairs, I saw a repost on Instagram from @thesecret365 and it was a list of things that one should promise themselves, like:

- I promise myself to be strong…
- To look at the sunny side of everything…
- To think only of the best…
- To forget the mistakes of the past and press on to the greater achievements of the future
- To give so much time improving myself that I have no time to criticize others
- To be too large for worry…
- To live in the faith that the whole world is on my side, so long as I am true to the best that is in me

After reading this I felt like maybe I had been missing all the good things that had been happening in my life, relationship, at work, etc. And that I've often let the so-called terrible things take up too much space in my head and energy in my spirit to appreciate it all.

There's nothing like looking yourself in the mirror and accepting the truth and owning your stuff, mess, or whatever you want to call it. I had no problem doing that; in fact, I am harder on myself than anyone. I need to get my mind right, and I had to promise myself to be my best self and that's it.

TGIF

Today is *Friday, January 19, 2018* and I'm working from home today. Baltimore County Public Schools are closing early today, so the twins will be home a little after noon. I managed to get through most of my assignments in the morning, and when I picked the twins up from the bus stop, we went to our favorite bakery, Iced Gems, for cupcakes. Jonathan and I picked out three of our favorites. Janell doesn't like them, and I'll share with my husband if he wants one.

After that it was off to the Baltimore County Public Library for books to read for homework next week. Each night the twins must read for twenty minutes or more, and I figured they could pick up something different from what's on our bookshelves. We're starting to build our own library and I'm enjoying it. As a proud Amazon Prime Member, we love to order new books, and we get them in two days.

After a quick half-hour meeting early in the afternoon, I tuned in to CNN to see where things were with the possibility of the government shutting down. By 4:00 p.m., things didn't seem positive and that countdown clock on the screen didn't help any. The last time we were shut down was in 2013, and I can remember it like it was yesterday. In fact, we have Facebook memories to prove it. LOL. You got to love Facebook for their memories. I do!

I logged off before 6:00 p.m., and I swore I wouldn't spend too much time worrying about what the outcome would be. Because either way, I would just have to deal with it. Afterward, we ordered Papa Johns, tuned into Netflix, and binged on our favorite shows season after season. Then I gathered everyone from the basement and we headed upstairs. I was so beat that I fell asleep and didn't even know whether we were shut down or not. Until the next morning.

An early morning alert on my iPhone confirmed that the United States federal government shutdown of 2018 begins at midnight EST *Saturday, January 20, 2018*. Oh well, it is what it is.

Every couple of weeks, I must post this message on my Instagram: I need a huge amount of money!

I'm feeling like that this weekend.

I Can't

Here's a list of a few of the things I've felt like I can't deal with over the past few days…

I can't listen to any sad news, so-called "Fake News," etc.

I can't believe the president uses Twitter like he does.

I can't worry about if the government shuts down.

I can't figure out how the field mice keep getting in the house.

I can't take another sleepless night due to these damn night sweats.

I can't go to the hair salon right now; I'll sit in my own vanity chair.

I can't stand the way Microsoft Word skips through your damn document—typing this book has been a challenge.

I can't go to the grocery store or Dollar General this week; I'm sick of shopping for food and household items.

I can't wash another damn load of laundry.

I can't make my neighbors park straight, and stop them from putting their trash out on non-trash-days

I can't keep worrying about my book sales, or lack thereof.

I can't believe all these unarmed black men keep getting shot and killed by police officers!

I can't fix everything and everybody!

Government Shutdown

*M*onday, *January 22, 2018*. For the past few weeks, the federal government has been working under a Continuing Resolution due to a standoff between the president and Congress and between political parties.

We all had to report to work today to receive our official "furlough" paperwork. My husband was at work, and the kids were in school. I was working from home on Friday because the kids were sick last week. So, I called in for the meeting.

The meeting was short and quick. Once I received my official paperwork via email, I was to logoff and wait until the government was back open for business.

The Spot

I called my friend and coworker Amelia and told her we should meet up at The Spot! She called another friend/coworker, and we were on our way. I couldn't wait…

It's been awhile since we've been there, but I knew that it would feel like we'd been there yesterday. I got there first and when I walked in I saw at least one familiar face that instantly made me smile. My friend Jimmie. One of the first times we went to The Spot Jimmie and I sang karaoke together, "Fire and Desire" by Rick James and Tina Marie. It was awesome, and I knew we'd be friends forever. I was looking around for the bartender, so I could order my martini, but she was selecting music on the jukebox. Once she finished making her selections, she hooked me up!

Amelia came through next, and we ordered her drink and then some wings and fries. I had a feeling we would be in here for a while. The usual greetings from our friends at The Spot are great big hugs, and I was glad because hugs are always good.

While we waited for our friend Sherice, I selected a few more songs on the jukebox along with a newfound friend. I can't remember his name because that's what happens after two martinis from The Spot. But hopefully, I'll see him again. Several more friends arrive, and we are just laughing and loving life. Then we meet a new guy...His name is Mr. Garland—like Judy! Those were his exact words, not mine. Now I bet you're probably wondering, *how you can remember his name, but not the guy you selected fifteen songs with?* Well, that's because Mr. Garland—who we shortened as "G"—told us several times.

Mr. "G" enlightened us with his funny stories and account of his world travels. He even offered to take us on a trip anywhere we wanted to go. So, we began to ask ourselves where we wanted to go. Well, Paris sounded good to me, so there it was. Amelia was on board, and once Sherice arrived she was too. We enjoyed laughing and talking with Mr. G and hope to see him again. We finished up our drinks and food, and now it was time to go. Amelia headed out first. I looked over at Sherice, and she was yawning. A quick bathroom run for me and we're out! Yup, another eventful night at The Spot!

On the way home, I thought about how much fun we had at The Spot (Hertsch's Tavern) over the years.

When we first started going to The Spot, the bartender there used to make the most killer drinks that would knock a two-hundred-pound man down to his knees! I mean, the drinks weren't just cheap, but they were plentiful. My limit was two drinks and that was it, and those had to be chased down by an entire 16 oz. Bottle of water, and I had to smoke a flavored cigar! Shit.

I'll never forget a bunch of us went to The Spot to celebrate Amelia's birthday. I had been dieting around that time, drinking greens and cutting back. Well, by the time it was all said and done, I hadn't eaten a lot but chugged down more than my allotted two drinks. I sang karaoke per usual, took a taste of birthday cake, and knew something wasn't right. I made my way to the bathroom and slid right on down the wall. Vomit in my weave and all over the floor! Yuk, I was carried out and driven home. Then to make matters worse, the same thing happened to another friend. The next day, I was hungover and felt so embarrassed, and I apologized profusely to the birthday girl. She understood, and I am thankful she and her friends were there to help me.

We don't go to The Spot much anymore, but when we do it's like we never left. It's the only place we can go in the heat of summer, play Christmas songs, and have the whole place singing like it's December. For old times' sake, I hope we can make it there again soon. I'm in need of a good martini, loud jukebox, random hugs, and just an enjoyable time.

Tuesday, January 23, 2018. The shutdown ended last night so it's back to work today, but from home; and in the office tomorrow.

Dinner Jazz Radio

*T*hursday, January 25, 2018. I'm so glad today was a work-from-home day. It was so hard for me go into the office yesterday. After working almost thirty years, it's normal to feel that way. Sometimes I still can't believe I've been working over half my life.

Once I finished all my meetings and shut down for the day, it was time to divert all my attention to the twins. First up was homework. The usual single daily sheet, and then the completion of weekly homework packet.

My son was gone for a minute to go to the barbershop for a haircut, and my daughter was enjoying her time alone, so she could watch YouTube and play her games on her tablet. Meanwhile, I was preparing dinner. Tonight, was Purdue *Italian Style* chicken breasts (they gave me an extra one in the pack) with linguini and green beans. Yummy. I don't know about anyone else, but I am looking forward to dinner tonight.

Once the guys returned home, I started to enforce that homework had to be completed by 6:30 p.m. so we would be on schedule for baths, etc. But no, everybody was procrastinating because I had stopped to gather the recycling.

Finally, it was time for dinner. For once I wanted to hear someone ask me, "What's for dinner?" but they didn't. Instead, once everyone sat down they just had blank looks on their faces as if to say, "What's this?"

I had a special treat for dinner tonight as well. Usually I turn off the television when we eat to stop one of the kids from turning away from the table conversation, or even worse, getting up to go in the living room to listen or see up close. Tonight, I thought we could listen to some "Dinner Jazz Radio" courtesy of Pandora. And I am so glad I did. Talk about a break from the norm! The kids didn't appreciate it, but I knew they liked it. We will do this again.

Talk Less

I couldn't believe my ears when someone very dear to me told me that I should "talk less." Like really, right in the middle of a somewhat serious conversation you would say that to me. But you know what? I'm glad they did. Because now I know that that is exactly what I need to do with them. Talk less and act more! Message received and roger that!

But you know just like anything else, sometimes we say things we don't mean. Or words that we choose come back to bite us. I don't think we set out to intentionally hurt the ones we love, but a lot of times that's exactly what ends up happening. This year I am going to try my best not to hurt the ones I love.

Talk less—As I worked from home today, I felt the urge to reach out and call that person, but I didn't. Instead, I sent a text message giving a few examples of things that I felt that we *needed* to talk about. I was hoping for a response, but there was none. Why? Were you at a loss for words today, but so sharp with the tongue the day before? Oh, why do I bother *to keep* wracking my brain trying to make logic out of other people's thoughts and words?

Talk less—I don't want to talk less with you, but I guess I'll have to. Thank goodness for family and friends, huh? Oh, I guess I should talk less to them too? Let me tell you something, if I didn't *talk* to *someone* about the some of the shit I go through and how I feel, I would probably go insane. Or shake the shit out of someone.

I've been told that I live in "a fantasy world." But I'm not. I'm just hoping for the best, wishing we could change and just be happy! Learn how to apologize right away and move past things. Why do we drag things out so long? Every time it hurts more and more. And it takes something away.

More action—Like getting out of the kitchen and sitting down to write these pages tonight. I feel great, but tomorrow will be better because I will go and sit my pretty self on a barstool somewhere and say, "I'll have a martini, please!"

The Big 9

Today is *Monday, January 29, 2018* and our twins are nine years old! We are truly blessed. There's no big party planned for this year; instead, the four of us are going to hang out and do whatever the twins want to do.

They wanted to stay home from school today, but I negotiated for an "early dismissal" instead. And when my husband came home, we were heading out for some family fun and then to dinner.

First up was Players Fun Zone in Westminster, Maryland. We practically had the place to ourselves since it was a weekday. They bounced, crashed bumper cars, and then we teamed up for some family friendly laser tag. Before we left, they had played games and won some prizes.

Now I was guessing they would want to take advantage of us telling them they could go wherever they wanted for their birthday and would choose McDonald's or Chick-Fil-A, but not our kids. They wanted to go to Bonefish Grill. Bang-Bang shrimp here we come, and oh a Hawaiian martini for Mommy!

I hope they will always remember the fun they had with Mommy and Daddy on their ninth birthday, and I look forward to planning their tenth in a few months. It's going to be one for the books—double-digit birthdays here we come!

Lo Loestrin

I t's *Wednesday, January 31, 2018* and guess what happened to me first damn thing? Yup, my cycle. Well, this month I am trying out this low-dose birth control in hopes of shortening my menstrual cycles and helping with the perimenopausal symptoms. I certainly don't have to worry about getting pregnant, thank goodness.

Besides, whenever I joke with the family about having another baby, they give me a thumb down. Guess that's that. And guess what else is over? My thirty days. So there, if you want to know more about me, then follow me on my social media accounts or send me an email or something. But this is it!

Aunt Dot has officially taken over, so before I get all emotional and stuff (that's possible during this time), I'm moving on. See, I've concluded that "most" women only have one good week in the month. That is the two weeks after/before their cycle. The week before is no good because you're gearing up for your cycle to come (sanitary products, cravings), and then when it does that's it. Let me warn you ladies, DO NOT make any life-altering decisions during this week. The week after, you're recuperating and catching up on sleep, sex, and extracurricular activities. So, take advantage of that "good week" two weeks before your cycle. Thank me later!

The rest of the book is me giving you my random thoughts and feelings, or as I call them daily #hashtags. Oh, and I will include some poetry.

PART II

HASHTAGS

#Girlfriends

I have a handful of ladies that I can honestly call my girlfriends and that I am glad to know. Over the years, we have been through it all together. My longest friendship is with my friend Trenita, and it goes back to middle school. We have fond memories together, like when we took the train to Atlantic City, NJ for our first trip to a casino when we turned 21; and our first vacation out of the country to the Bahamas. I can always count on her to plan a girl's trip for us, and to calm me down when I get riled up.

It seems like yesterday that my friend Margot was teaching me how to drive in her Nissan Z28 and taking me to get my driver's license. When I started working for the federal government in 1986, Angela was the first person I met, and she showed me everything I needed to know to hold down that personnel office. She also told me that it's important to understand how to back your car into a parking spot-Thank You Angie!

Then there's Shawn, Quandra, and Cynthia, who were mothers when we were in our twenties; and at the time I couldn't fathom going through what they did at that age. I used to call my friend Shawn, and almost every time she would be doing laundry. For the life of me, I couldn't figure out why, but now I know with a family of four you'll have endless laundry. I don't mind when Shawn nicely tells me, "You have issues," or when I am telling Cynthia something funny about the twins, and she responds, "Uh, uh." Their children have grown now, and mine are in elementary school. However, we are still there for each other.

Friends are necessary. They help hold you accountable for things and let you know when you're out of order and wrong. I don't know what I would do without my good friend Amelia whom I have spent endless hours with on the phone laughing, sometimes crying, and just lending each other an ear. She will tell me quick, "First of all," or "Listen" with that distinct New York accent and I know she's serious.

A devoted friend will tell you the truth! She won't always agree with what you say and do, but she will at least hear you out. Like my friend Quandra. We met at the bus stop after work one day and have been friends ever since. I can also thank her for introducing me to my husband. One thing is for sure with Quandra, I can always count on that Pisces to give it to me straight, and I appreciate that! We used to go out the night of daylight savings so we could get that extra hour in at the club. We used to run the clubs and have a ball, and then it just got old. I felt so honored when she and her husband asked me to be their daughters, Godmother.

Your girlfriends play many roles in your life sometimes, and some may even be more than one of them. Some are like a second mother. Some of them are like the sisters you wish you had or not. My aunt Lois and I are close in age, and she is a Scorpio. We are a lot alike, and she understands me. Some get on your nerves and drive you crazy. Some of them bring your spirits up and make you laugh when you're down. I know I get on their nerves, but I don't care. Well, I do, but I still call them, text them to death, tag them on funny posts on Instagram, most definitely talk their ears off, and the ones I work with, I will stop by their offices at work. Now, it's all about family with all of us, as it should be. I'm grateful and honored to have had these ladies as my friends for as long as I have, and I look forward too many more years.

Here's to "Girlfriends!" I'll have a martini, please!

#MidlifeCrisis

I s there such a thing as a "midlife crisis"? According to Pinterest, yes and no. In my opinion, as soon as I turned forty-five, "something" happened to me. Whether or not I want to put crisis before or after it depends on how you look at it. That year I started having hot flashes and night sweats, and my menstrual cycle was all out of whack. So much so that my OB/GYN midwife thought I might be pregnant. I was like, well if I am, I'm going to own Johns Hopkins Hospital because I don't even have all my lady parts anymore okay!

Nevertheless, I walked away that year with a new Rx for those forty-five-year-old symptoms. But that didn't last long. Within six months, I threw those Clonidine's away! I had decided that I was going to sweat it out and deal with all the irregularities, try to get some loving when I can and keep it moving.

Now men, on the other hand, I truly believe they go through a goddamn midlife crisis. One month they want a new hot rod car, the next month they want to move to a bigger house, and then the next season they want to stay put. But I am not mad, because hell, so do we! And if we must deal with their little crises, they need to be ready to deal with whatever we bring. Because one thing is for sure and two things are for certain, that my ass might wear five different wigs in one week. To keep up with me, you better #StayReady so you won't have to #GetReady

#UFTs and #IVF

When I look in the mirror and see the 6 inch scar on my belly, I think about when I first discovered I had Uterine Fibroid Tumors (UFT). I was twenty-eight years old, and in the best shape of my life. Then I started having the worst menstrual cramps. If that wasn't enough, I had excessive bleeding during my cycle, and sometimes I would look like I was pregnant. What was going on? I went to my gynecologist, and he scheduled me for an ultrasound. The ultrasound showed that I had two uterine fibroid tumors each about the size of small grapefruits. He explained to me that they were benign and recommended that I have surgery to remove them if they continued to cause me discomfort and if I wanted to have children. After doing some research, and getting a second opinion, I scheduled my myomectomy to remove the tumors.

Having the surgery was one of the best decisions I have made, as I felt so much relief afterward. Also, my menstrual cycles were better, and the days of seven to ten days of bleeding were over. For a few years at least. Yup, you guessed it, by the time I was ready to settle down and start a family (2006 to 2007), the fibroids returned—and with a vengeance.

Although I was able to conceive naturally, the fibroids caused me to miscarry. The fetus was growing but was in my fallopian tube, which resulted in an ectopic pregnancy and its removal. I was devastated. I knew that this would further hinder my ability to conceive, and when I left the Greater Baltimore Medical Center with the shell they had given me (to represent my fetus) I wasn't sure if I wanted to try again.

Because this happened before I was married, a part of me felt and believed that it was God's way of telling me to do this right. So shortly after we were married, my husband and I sought help from the Johns Hopkins (JH) Fertility Center. After in-depth consultation and multiple testing, we agreed to try in vitro fertilization or IVF, but first I would have to undergo another myomectomy to remove the fibroids.

Going through the IVF process was informative and emotional. I felt confident with Dr. Garcia and his staff, but after two failed cycles, I thought my body was giving up. So, we decided to take a break for a few months before the third and final try. After our third cycle, we were successful and expected twins. I thank God and the doctors at JH and would recommend anyone to them for help with their fertility needs.

Almost ten years later, the fibroids are back, and again I am faced with whether to have them removed or live with them forever.

#PeoplePleasing

I didn't make any 2018 New Year's resolutions; however, one thing that I will NOT do too much of this year is trying to please everybody. Nope, this year I am working on satisfying Tamara first…me, myself, and I. Now don't get me wrong, I know that I can't make any "major decisions" without considering my family (husband and children) first, but in general, I'm doing ME! It's been too many years that I have been putting my wants and needs on the back burner trying to please everybody, and for what? For their asses to be ungrateful and not appreciate it. Besides, I've been people pleasing the last decade or more, and it has been like riding on an old wooden roller coaster, wild and rough. Now I'm ready for some smooth sailing.

#RESPECT!

I know everybody heard Bird Man when he was at the Breakfast Club and said, "Put some respect on my name!" So, you all realize he meant that with every bit of New Orleans he had in him, and guess what? I respect him for it!

"Don't let someone get comfortable disrespecting you." Also, you shouldn't get comfortable disrespecting someone either. There were many times when I felt disrespected and felt like I was reciprocating that same behavior. That wasn't a good feeling. I mean I had started talking myself into believing that "sometimes" this was how relationships were, and this was how people who "love" each other behave. However, it didn't feel right.

The lies over the years were so outrageous, who do they think I am, Boo Boo the Fool! My best guy friends used to tell me how cute I was and how much of a great catch I was, but I didn't believe them. I started doubting myself and accepting a lot. I had to tell myself that I was more deserving of better relationships and that I was capable of being and doing more as a woman.

When I was single, I would put up with some stuff, my good girlfriends used to say, "more than they ever would," but eventually I would break it off. And not look back. Now that I'm married, it's not that simple. You can't, or shouldn't, walk away because you're mad or you're not getting your way, but what do you do?

Respect goes both ways, and when you're in a relationship both parties must be willing to do the work and make it work! After all, if you admire someone and hold them in high regard, it shouldn't be that hard. Try to understand each other's point of view and feelings, and most of all remember that COMMUNICATION is critical!

#TrustYourGut

This year, I made some promises to myself. One was always to trust my gut. There have been too many instances where I did the opposite and paid dearly for doing so. When something doesn't feel right, it usually isn't. TRUST YOUR GUT!

#LiveLoveLaugh

Thank God, I have a sense of humor! Otherwise, I would have killed someone or at least shaken the shit out of them. My friend Herman and I used to call it the "Adult Shaken Syndrome"; it was necessary for some people. When they say that one thing, ask you that one question, instead of answering them you grab them by their shoulders and give them three to five quick, but firm shakes.

As I embrace my forty-eighth year of life, there are too many days where I sit and ask myself "could've, should've, would've." If I had to do it all over again, I would've gone to college RIGHT after high school, and I should've had children earlier because at least I would've been able to keep up with them better then. Working out would've been a "way of life," and my diet would've been too! Right now, I'm living with degenerative arthritis in my knees, fluid on my knees, sprained ankles, and the aches and pains oh my! Damnit…the last three years have been very trying on my body and emotionally draining. I've been feeling less attractive and insecure. Although I know I'm beautiful and sexy, the mind can play tricks on you.

Because I have a sense of humor, now I laugh about many things that used to make me cry. Like my hair today, I can genuinely say that I am "Bald and Beautiful" with or without my wigs.

#BenefitoftheDoubt

I *always* give the benefit of the doubt. No matter who or what the situation, I try to first let the person prove themselves. Especially with my family. Like the time I discovered that my Kindle was cracked and broken. I asked my husband and the twins what happened, and I got one set of three words that I don't want to hear. "I don't know." So, nobody in the damn house knew how Mommy's Kindle got broken? But looks like everybody's tablets are working. Okay, that's how we are living now. All right. Noted.

One day I took a survey and asked a few of my friends to give two words that described me. Surprisingly, almost all of them gave "nice" as one of the words. Hmmm, "nice." Was I nice to people? I didn't expect most of them to say nice. I felt like sometimes I could be a smart ass, and I enjoyed being sarcastic as often as possible. But, apparently, I'm nice. Some of the other words used to describe me were smart, sexy, independent, strong, feisty, humble, funny, chatty, approachable, and dependable.

My husband says that I am too "emotional" and that I shouldn't take everything so personal. Well, I don't take everything personally, but words from him, I did! And no one could make me feel worse than my kids, especially when they cry and if I feel like I have disappointed them. Oh, my goodness! Do they give me the benefit of the doubt because I'm Mommy and I'm so nice? Regardless, the consensus is that I am a nice person, so I'll take that.

#Pandora

When life gets me down, I listen to music. Pandora at home and my iTunes in the car and many nights before I go to bed. My family should know by now what kind of mood I'm in by the type of music I play. First, when I'm happy "Mon, it's Bob Marley." If I'm going through relationship issues, then I'm going with Sade (old school) Mary J. Blige, or now my favorites are Jhene Aiko, SZA, and H.E.R. (I still don't know what she looks like or what the letters stand for, but it's okay). Songs like "Focus" and "Lights On" touch me. Please take a minute and listen to her, and I'm going to hum it. "Wish you would just focus on me; can you focus on me? Baby, can you focus on me, on me, baby focus, can't you see, I just want to love you, baby, look me in my eyes." See, there's that word again— LOVE!

When I'm feeling a little thuggish or hardcore, then it's time for some Lil' Kim, Nicki Minaj, or Cardi B.

"Said, Lil bitch, you can't fuck with me if you wanted to." Say no more, fam, say no more. When I am feeling gorgeous, I tune into Plies (I love that Southern drawl that man got, I swear). Future can take me somewhere when I'm smoking I can't lie. Also, Drake is an absolute must when I have my favorite glass of wine.

"I'll have a martini please!" when I'm listening to R Kelly (12 play) or Beyoncé (Speechless). You cannot tell me that I am not Sasha motherfucking Fierce wearing a diamond shirt! Baby, I wore that song out one night in Karaoke. You couldn't tell me that I wasn't a star.

#Cubicle Therapy

Sometimes at work, I venture out of my cubicle to chat and laugh out loud with coworkers. Right now, we have a vacant cubicle in our area, and I often joke about how we should convert it to our "lounge" or "therapy space." Now our office is majority women, and we have three good men. We call ourselves divas, and they are our divos.

Most of the ladies in the office have older children so I will ask them about child-rearing situations, school scenarios, and for the veteran wives, suggestions on how to handle relationship problems. There are also a few single folks in the office and younger ones as well. For the most part, the work environment is tolerable. However, I enjoy having the option of working from home twice a week. It's a good break from the monotony.

There are times when I feel like it's a bit risky to talk about personal and private matters in the workplace. I mean we're friends, but we're also coworkers. There's a distinction that comes into play at the most inopportune time. Also, there is the risk of what you've said being used against you or shared with others. I guess that's a chance you must take, and I have.

Let's face it, some of us spend up to ten hours a day at the workplace. That may be more time than you spend with your family on weekdays. We have formed friendship and bonds, and most often you have a genuine concern for your coworkers. It's nice when everyone can be sincere and honest with each other, instead of fake and phony. Although none of us are "therapists," I believe that most of us value each other's opinion as women, mothers, and wives. Conversations with our divos prove to be beneficial as well. Since there's so many of us in the office, it's refreshing to get a man's point of view sometimes.

#Bed-wetting

When I was a child, I wet the bed for years. I didn't know why, and I couldn't help myself. I used to get in trouble for it, sometimes spanked. My mother used to limit what I drank and the time I drank it, but I would still wet the bed. What was most embarrassing was spending the night away from home (like at Grandma's) and wetting the bed. I had to sleep on the rollaway cot, which sucked because at some point someone else may have to sleep on it as well. But I couldn't help it.

As an adult, I researched bed-wetting and read somewhere that it was hormonal for some people. There, that settled it. I was satisfied with that and didn't consider it a minute further. Within the last ten years, I have occasionally wet the bed because of what I drank. Yup, I'm straight blaming it on the alcohol. Rum to be specific. Mind you, when this would happen, I would jump up out of the bed frantic, in a panic to #FIXIT right away.

However, when I was in that sleep zone, I would really be thinking that I was in the bathroom, on the toilet, and doing the right thing. I mean one time I woke up and had even pulled up my nightgown. When I told my girlfriends about this, some of them said this has happened to them as well, so now I don't feel so bad.

It's been a while since this has happened, but I can see myself jumping up (my husband too), stripping the sheets and comforter off all in one snatch, putting the fan on (it stays posted up in the bedroom since the night sweats), and running down to the basement to throw all of that in the washing machine. By the time I would get back upstairs, my husband would be back in bed on his side, sound asleep!

#BathroomRules

There is nothing that will set me off quicker than someone in the family breaking the "Bathroom Rules." To help enforce these rules, I found the perfect wall art at Bed Bath & Beyond for my bathroom and placed it over the towel rack. The list reads as follows;

Bathroom Rules

- Wash Your Hands
- Hang Up Your Towel
- Brush & Floss
- Clean Up After Yourself
- Put the Seat Down
- Always Use Soap
- Pick Up Your Clothes
- Don't Forget to Flush
- Turn Off the Lights

I have made it clear to the family that in my mind

there is no reason for any of them not to follow these rules, and if/when they don't, believe me, there will be dire consequences. Yup, and I'm probably going to yell out loud!

Also, another thing, does anyone else still pull the shower curtain back to make sure no killer is hiding in the tub? When I stumble into the bathroom in the wee hours of the morning, I still remember to do that! #toomanymurdermysteries

#SecondTimeAround

For those of you who don't know, this is my second book. My first book is titled, I Love Hate My Hair (My Journey with Alopecia). It was a short story about just that, my journey with alopecia. I have no regrets about sharing my story about my hair loss, in fact, since I did, I have met more people who have alopecia. As I scroll down Instagram, I see more men coming forward talking about and showing how they deal with their hair loss; and the so many awesome Stylists who create #manweaves and hair units for them.

But on the flip side of that, I also have some folks who say things like, "Why don't you just shave it off sis?" You're pretty enough. I simply reply, "Because I don't want to." And I think there are thousands of other women who don't want to either. Everyone has their own opinion about what you should do. I wonder what they would do if they were in our shoes.

I wasn't sure how to promote the book or anything. I got suggestions from the publisher on how to target my audience, but it was harder than I thought. So, I just did what I thought was natural—start with family and friends and individuals whom I knew had hair loss issues. Promote on social media, and I also attended the Baltimore Book Festival.

Although I haven't sold many books on Amazon or Barnes and Noble, I do sell when I go out at vending events. Also, there have been a few sales where I mailed the book to folks who don't like to buy online. Reviews came into me by way of phone calls, texts, and emails. I only received two online, and they were both excellent. It's hard to get customers to go online and give reviews, but I am grateful. Thankful for everyone who purchased the book and took the time to read it.

I'm going to try a different approach with this book, so we'll see how it goes. Either way, I'm going to keep writing. Why, because I love it.

#SincerelyIncarcerated

Iwould have never in a million years thought that I would have relatives who would be in prison for the rest of their lives. Take a minute and imagine that. The possibility of never coming home again. Or never waking up in your bed, instead, being confined to a 6x8 feet prison cell. Not being able to go outside when you want to or cook your favorite meal. Not going to your job anymore or never driving your car again. Having to resort to occasional visits from friends and family instead of hugs, kisses, and being with them is just too much to fathom.

I have two relatives incarcerated now, and both will more than likely spend the rest of their natural lives in prison. That bothers me. I hurt for them, and I try my best to help them in any way that I can. However, not everyone feels that way. A lot of people think the total opposite, especially when it isn't the incarcerated family members first go-round. Now I'm not judging anyone or trying to tell them what to do. I am expressing how I feel.

I do what I do for them because I love them, and they are family. Sometimes I also feel like their incarceration has somehow become part of my life. But what if it were me? And I was in prison. I would hope someone would look out for me anyhow. There is a saying that with every action there is a consequence. At the end of the day, after the judge or jury has made their decision, whether you're innocent or guilty has no bearing. Once that gavel drops and the judge sentences, that's it.

When I receive a letter from them or accept their collect calls, I can hear the relief in their voices. The joy from someone picking up and allowing them to communicate with the outside world or to express what they're feeling about their circumstances. I read the letters, and they reveal what they need, hesitant to ask because they don't want to be a burden. Or how inquisitive they are about what's going on with the rest of the family and me. And man, they will see my face because I plan to visit.

One of them has been away for over ten years now, and I have never visited at the facility he is at now. But for years I visited him at other facilities and have always been there for him. Writing letters and sending birthday and Father's Day cards. Putting money on his phone account so he can call me and others. See sometimes they need to hear our voices and connect with the outside world.

If you have a loved one incarcerated, try to give them support if you can. If not monetarily, then write a letter, send pictures of you and the family, or give them your phone number so they can call you sometimes. Today, some prisons don't allow you to send greeting cards anymore, which is unfortunate. But that's the way it is.

There are also support groups for families of prisoners and resources for spouses and children of prisoners. For specific information on the policies, contact the facility directly to make sure you understood what is allowed and expected of you when visiting.

#FOE

Family over Everything! Is that just another hashtag, or does this have bearing anymore? I'm not sure. My father is deceased; however, I sit down sometimes with a drink and smoke and I talk with him via his urn and picture. I light a candle for him, and I make sure to wish him a happy New Year, happy birthday, happy Father's Day, happy Thanksgiving, a Merry Christmas. And I keep him abreast of what's going on in the family. Why? I don't know. It just feels like the right thing to do.

I talk to my mother every day. She's my best friend. I can't imagine not speaking to her, not visiting her, not getting a hug and kiss from her. And the only times that I've been angry or mad with her was because we disagreed with something involving other members of the family. When I was a child, I was the oldest, so I took up for my brothers at times. That carried on into our adulthood, and I would take up for them and get mad at Mommy when she didn't do what they wanted her to do. But then I realized that she had good reason not to.

Or when I was five years old, and she had left my father, and we moved from one apartment building to the next (in the same complex). I told him where our new place was. I was a kid, and I didn't know any better, but when I was older, I understood why my mother had to leave him, and it was for the better. These situations made us stronger, and we have a bond that is like no other. Growing up with teenage parents was a struggle, but it made me appreciate everything we had. I also knew that I didn't want to live that same struggle. So, I waited and waited before marrying and starting a family. But guess what? Life is sometimes still a struggle. Are we ever prepared? At what age are you ready to settle down and start a family?

I haven't spoken with some members of my family now for over a year. Initially, I was hurt, cried, and even thought about making amends. But when I think about the core of the problem, and it stems from disrespect, I can't. I won't mend, and I won't break to apologize or attempt to downsize my feelings about individuals who want to be catered to and think the world owes them something. Grow up. Know that everything is not going to go your way, and guess what? Nobody owes you anything!

Last year, I almost came to blows, a physical fight, with someone! I couldn't believe it. I haven't had a "fight" since middle school. Why had I let these individuals take me out of character like that? Or was that who I was? I certainly didn't go and plan to bring bodily harm to anyone, but I certainly wasn't going to stand still and let anyone harm me, my family, and never my mother!

My daughter and I went to Bed Bath & Beyond, for no other reason than the fact that I got another coupon in the mail. I love that store. And after walking around looking at all the beautiful pillows, towels, and picture frames, she wanted me to buy a wall plaque that merely said: **FAMILY IS EVERYTHING!**

#Homebased Businesses

Two years ago, I became an It Works! Distributor. What was supposed to be a quick trip to the Columbia Mall to buy body wraps turned into a $99-plus investment. Now I told the representative there I wasn't interested, but I let her give me the speech. The spiel about how "it works" and what a great business plan it was, and how easy it was to make money. Yeah, for her maybe. But all I wanted to do was buy some body wraps to help me fit into some random outfit I wanted to wear.

I have worked home-based businesses before. Amway back in the 90s and Mary Kay in the early 2000s, but I quit. And the main reason I did was that I couldn't find people to support me. Not buying the products, but to join my team, you know, work the business with me. They didn't mind buying products from me, but they didn't want to join the company.

That was a deterrent for me, but I still signed up with It Works! I proceeded with caution this time, especially vowing not to be stuck with a bunch of products that I wouldn't be able to sell. I had my launch party, ordered supplies, and even got a car magnet, which somebody stole! Was that a sign? Should I have followed my gut feeling and not signed up to be a distributor?

Now the pressure was on. Not only did I have to sell this product, but I had to look the part. I mean, how could I sell body wraps and greens and fat fighters when according to my BMI I was obese? No matter how good you might think I look, at 5'2" and weighing over 150 pounds (I will not divulge my exact weight), I was not qualified to talk to anyone about getting into shape.

Soon enough, I had my four loyal customers, and they seemed to like the products and used them regularly. Seeing results, they wanted to try more. But no one was interested in signing up to be a distributor and join my team. That's what was missing, and that's where the money is, my friends. I can have twenty loyal customers, but it would be better if I had four or five distributors to go along with them.

The fact that no one wanted to join my team discouraged me, and I just quit on It Works! Again. I haven't placed an order for myself in months, nor have I tried to sell or order any products. I feel bad about it sometimes, especially when the distributor that I signed with still includes me in her group messages on Facebook or tags me on something in Messenger. Why haven't they given up on me? I haven't shown any initiative at all. My guess is because this is their livelihood, and they have seen how the business can work for them. I may listen on a Sunday to the weekly call, and I'll tell you why.

I keep hearing about the need to have multiple streams of income, and I know these companies can and do work if you put your mind to it and do the job. I hadn't done the work because I was too busy "working" for the government and "doing" for my family.

I realize that I must create multiple streams of income for myself, and this may be one to reconsider.

#SelfieOfTheDay

How did the selfie start? Oh no sense in guessing, let me check Google. Okay, so here's what I found: "Australia has proudly laid claim to inventing the term 'selfie'—named 2013 word of the year by Oxford Dictionary—after its first-known use was revealed to be by an Australian describing a photograph taken while drunk at a 21st birthday party."[1] And there's more "Robert Cornelius Self-Portrait: The First Ever 'Selfie'" (1893). Oxford Dictionary defines a selfie as a "photograph that one has taken of oneself, typically one taken with a smartphone or webcam and uploaded to a social media website."[2]

Well, I want to thank Mr. Cornelius and the Australian personally... Thinking back on before we used

---

1 https://www.telegraph.co.uk/news.worldnews/australiaandthe-pacific/australia/10459115/Australian-man-invented-the-selfie-after-drunken-night-out.html
2 https://publicdomainreview.org/collections/robert-cornelius-self-portrait-the-first-ever-selfie-1839/

smartphones, we were taking pictures with Polaroid instant cameras. We weren't turning them to ourselves to take selfies; we were aiming them at someone or something else. Nevertheless, you can count on me to post one on my Instagram page at least once a week, and whoever doesn't like it can Unfollow, Delete, or Like.

Today, I look forward to logging in to Twitter to see what the trending topics are, and to see what POTUS is thinking. LOL. Love him or hate him, you must know what the president is thinking. And the best way to do so is to follow his tweets. I'm hoping I will never wake up and read a tweet from him like, "We're going to war!" Yikes, that scares the shit out of me.

#MiniMe

You ever get mad at your kids because they're just like you? I mean most days my little girl does something that makes me want to scream. However, I can't because I can see myself in her A LOT! Like just now she's walking around moping with her head down because I told her to put some clothes on. It's freezing, and she can't walk around the house half-dressed. However, no, she must be defiant. So then when Daddy calls, she tells on me. Can you believe that?

Kids are smarter than we think they are, and master manipulators, but I'm not going for it. Also, I told my husband that we CANNOT let her pit us against each other. When I tucked them into sleep last night, my daughter and I talked about how we would pray to the "snow fairy" so they could stay home tomorrow. Sure enough, the fairies answered our prayers! Due to inclement weather, most schools closed today, and I had the option of working from home. Thank goodness. I always take off when this happens because my work schedule is more flexible.

Today baby girl and I had a blast. Coffee and yogurt in bed while watching the news. Then it was time for me to get up and log on. I worked through my emails and accomplished a lot. Then at lunchtime, we all went out to shovel and clean off the cars. After she was finished playing with her dolls, she worked on homework and then came and gave me the biggest hug, thanking me for praying to the fairy with her last night, and then for doing extraordinary things with her today. Sometimes it's okay to see yourself in someone else. Today was one of those days.

#WeddingBells

Many of my friends were married when we were in our 20s, and some of them are still going strong. Then again, some of them have married more than once. I used to feel like I was always the bridesmaid and never the bride. When my day finally came, I was thirty-eight years old. I was one of the few who was still single without kids. It was hard to convince myself that it was okay that I was. Today, I'm looking through my wedding photo album and thinking about that day 9-3-07 (that's how I had the date on our invitation).

We planned our wedding from start to finish. Working with the coordinator at the event space and counting on your wedding party and guests to act accordingly. When that day came, I was so excited, but tired from little sleep the night before. I was so anal that I had a PowerPoint presentation for every part of the day. I gave it to my mother when we arrived at the reception site and asked her to "double-check" everything to make sure it was right. Finally, the event coordinator insisted that I relinquish control and relax. I gathered all the ladies in the wedding party, and we held hands in a prayer circle. I prayed for "No surprises," but unbeknownst to me, they had plotted the opposite.

Oh well, c'est la vie! As my husband and I sat in front of our two hundred guests and watched everything unfold, he grabbed my knee and said, "It's okay, honey." Then right after that, the wedding coordinator informs me that they banned my father from the bar. How's that possible? It was an open bar. However, that didn't stop him; my uncle just went up and asked for two drinks every time. That day was one of the happiest and most stressful days of my life. However, almost everyone I know that attended said they had a ball! One of my coworkers said that her daughter, who was a teenager then, still talks about how much fun it was.

So, I guess that should make me feel better, huh? Well, it doesn't. By the end of that event, I had run up into the bridal suite to use the restroom and let out a silent cry. By the time the limousine took my husband and me back home, he reassured me that the day went well and that I shouldn't worry. So, it began "I'll have a martini please!"

#Time

You ever feel like you never have enough time? From the moment I wake up in the morning, I feel pressed for time. I've never been an early bird and probably never will be. But my husband gets up early, so I do! Then I try to go back to sleep until it's time to get the kids ready for school, but that rarely happens. Instead, I take the time to enjoy my cup of coffee and watch or listen to the news. Occasionally, I will throw a load in the washing machine, mop the kitchen floor, check homework, sign papers that must go back to school, or pay bills online. Whew! Why can't I lie back down? After all, I am still tired. But I don't.

Now it's time to wake the kids up, fix them breakfast, maybe pack lunch (depending on what's on the school menu), and then get our outfits ready. I know I can do that at night, but most of the time we don't. My son may have his outfits for the week, but it won't matter if my daughter and I do because more than likely we'll change our minds. Yup, I told you, she's my mini-me. Once they are up, the clock starts ticking because now I must make sure we eat, brush teeth, wash faces, get dressed, make sure everyone hair is straight, and get downstairs in time to pack those bookbags up. All this must be done so we can head out of the house by 8:00 a.m. to walk up to the bus stop.

I can't tell you how many mornings we missed this deadline and the bus. There are several reasons why, and I don't want to point any fingers as to who may be responsible more mornings than others. But it's usually not my son. I feel sorry for him most mornings because he's usually downstairs waiting for us to do that one last thing so that we can head out the door. Nevertheless, he's had perfect attendance this year, and my daughter has only been absent when she was sick. I feel horrible when they miss the bus, so I throw on my shoes and coat and drop them off. Once I get back in the house, if I'm not ready to go to work immediately, I grab a second cup of coffee and sit down to take a breath. You know what I mean if you're a mom of eight-year-old twins too!

I may sip that second cup of coffee as I have nowhere to go, but if it's one of the three days that I must be in the office, then the clock starts ticking again. Ugh…some mornings I give myself a pep talk to get ready quick! See, I've been working at the same place now for the past thirty-one years. So, some mornings it's hard for me. Don't get me wrong; I am grateful and all those other adjectives you can use to describe how you feel about having a job.

Usually, I manage to pull myself together to be ready to walk out by 9:30 a.m. Keep in mind that I must be there by 10:00 a.m. Getting there in thirty minutes is do-able; however, the traffic in our area can be tricky. Unless I'm aware of an accident or backup on the beltway, that is my preferred route. Otherwise, I will have to take the back roads and scenic route. I'm happy when I can arrive on time, but when I'm late, the clock starts to work against me. Then I'll have to take leave to get off earlier to pick up the twins from aftercare in the afternoon.

The afternoon/evening clock is too much, and I don't even want to get into it, but let's say that MOST of those nights I want a martini, please!

#SexDrugs&Alcohol

For those of us in our mid-40s, know that sex is different now. For some men, they must deal with erectile dysfunction (ED); God knows there are enough commercials for medication that can help them with it. With all the side effects of those drugs, I don't know who in their right mind would take any of that stuff. Also, for women, we may have vaginal dryness or lack of interest. Yup, that's true, and we have commercials too. So, what do we need to do, friends? Stock up on lubricants and watch more porn? Have more foreplay? Go to a swinger's club? What? What are you guys doing?

ED and perimenopausal symptoms are touchy subjects and often hard to come to grips with when there are problems in this area. When I first started having problems because of my perimenopausal symptoms, I felt like: "Not me!" I've never had this problem before, but then as I talked to some friends and older women, I realized that these symptoms were prevalent. I also consulted with my gynecologist, and she suggested prescription medication for my hot flashes and night sweats. She also recommended using lubricants, and now I'm taking birth control to help control my menstrual cycle. Geez, I thought my 20s were difficult. What's next?

A male friend of mine told me about this swingers' club in our area called Tabu Social Club, and he also sent me an invitation for my husband and me to check it out. I didn't even tell my husband about it. Instead, I just kept ordering stuff from Adam & Eve. Why? Because I love the FREE gifts, they send you when you order. Don't believe me? Go check it out for yourselves www.adameve. com. Right now, I'm waiting for a "Marie Pearl Choker & Lace Panties"!

#FlavoredCigars

I'm writing tonight around 6:00 p.m. while I have a few minutes alone. The television is on mute on CNN, and I'm listening to one of my favorite songs on iTunes. In the words of my girl Jhene Aiko: "Is it hot in here or is it just me? I'm so high in here from smoking all this weed... The only drug a bitch is on is a tree." (Sativa, Trip EP) I've been sipping some Ketel One with OJ, but some Sativa would be lovely right now.

I need some mellow downtime and these aching joints. I don't want to take any anti-inflammatories or muscle relaxers! Guess a Tylenol for arthritis will have to do, but you can best believe that I'm going to get a flavored cigar or something tomorrow! That's it, and that's all! #DontJudgeMe

Jhene's voice is angelic; I can feel her music. The beats are soft but heavy, and I love her freestyles. I saw her a few years ago at Rams Head in downtown Baltimore, and I hope to see her again soon. Take a #Trip (name of her latest EP) with her friends; I guarantee you won't regret it.

For the past few years, I have enjoyed going to the fiVe Martini Bar that was in Cockeysville, Maryland, but it's closed now. My friend Amelia turned me on to it, and most of the time I went with her, but there were a few occasions where I went alone. Charming place, not too big, friendly crowd, and a variety of different martinis on the menu with the best flat-bread pizza! We need to find a new martini Bar and fast.

#TheBanister

Does anyone else have about ten hoodies, shirts, jackets, or scarfs on their banister? We do, and no matter how many times I meticulously put everything back in its place they end up right back there. Why? During the Christmas holiday, I made a grand announcement that NO ONE BETTER NOT put anything on the banister while draped in fake garland and poinsettias. Except for one night, my family adhered to that one small rule.

#TheBedroomChair

O kay, as if the banister baggage wasn't enough, there's that bedroom chair that holds a weeks' worth of clothing. That's right, every night I unload my blouse or pants, sweater or jeans, and now a bathrobe on my vanity chair. This chair isn't that big and not adequate to hold all this stuff, but I do it. Also, in the morning when I'm trying to apply makeup and fix my wig, I sometimes sit on this stuff. Until I get so frustrated from looking at it, or very uncomfortable when I have that one longer-than-usual morning, and I take each piece and put it where it belongs. That place is usually the hamper. So why do I walk by it? Who knows? A habit I guess.

After my wash day, the chair is empty and pushed in, ready for the next week and load. This year I promised myself I would declutter every season and buy more storage bins and neatly stack and store my clothes, shoes, and accessories. However, until then, the vanity chair will continue to do its job and hold my stuff when I need it.

#Post-OperativeRecovery

These last few pages are to document the aftermath of my knee surgery (arthroscopy). As I mentioned, was scheduled for Wednesday, February 28 at 1:00 p.m. My husband went with me, and I was very nervous that morning. The twins were too.

When we arrived at the Ortho Maryland Surgical Center around noon, I was feeling relaxed and ready. I prayed to God that he would bless the minds and hands of the surgeons and staff and that the procedure would go well. After the formalities, tests, and paperwork it was time. Hubby kissed me, and the nurse rolled me into the operating room.

A few hours later and feeling "super relaxed" from the pain meds, I woke up in the recovery area talking with the nursing staff. They told me that the procedure went well and that they were going to get my husband so that we could leave shortly. The nurse helped me put on my gaucho pants and off we went, headed to Rite Aid to pick up my prescription pain meds and then home until it was time to pick up the twins.

Once we got home, I couldn't wait to lie back in the recliner and look around the living room like WTF. I was feeling a little bit of pain, and then I felt concerned suddenly about how I was going to manage the next few weeks.

Mom and Pop Pop came by with a bag of goodies to help with recovery. The bag had everything from soft cuddly socks, soup, and chocolate candy to crackers. Oh, and balloons. Before I made my way upstairs, we all grabbed something from the goody bag. I prepped for bath, ice pack, pain pills, and off to bed.

The next two days after surgery were challenging. I scooted down the stairs and took one foot at a time upstairs. I wore compression stockings during the day and took baby aspirin to make sure I didn't clot. Yeah, I'm good to go.

The family helped but encouraged me to do what I could for myself. I was like, "Umm, it's only Day 2 post-operation." Did I mention how hard it is for a Scorpio to deal with/live with a Gemini and two Aquarius? However, I succeed. By Saturday, I was going outside to go with my husband and son to take my daughter to her art class. It was the first day of her five-week course, and

I didn't want to miss meeting the instructor and checking out the classroom.

By Monday, February 26, I was back at Ortho Maryland for my follow-up with the surgeon and then in for my first session of physical therapy (PT). The doctor's appointment went well. I had my stitches removed; however, PT was a bit of a struggle. However, I was healthy and determined to get through this. I left there and had scheduled my PT for the next six weeks.

I started back to work the second week in March, but from home. I enjoyed working from home. The peace, not having to have small talk in the office, no traffic jams in the morning, or hustling and bustling to race from home to pick up the twins from aftercare.

Also, by this time I was out of the Hydrocodone. I looked down at the pill bottle and saw that it read: "NO REFILL." It turns out that I was able to manage without them. PT was helping, and the best part was the icing and TENS therapy afterward.

Some days I feel like I'm overdoing it, and I need to slow down. Other days I feel like I should be doing more. However, that's probably just my mind playing tricks on me. Having to juggle day-to-day activities is stressful, and with a diversion like surgery, it just adds to it. Shame on me for not being able to accept that I'm not at 100 percent and that I am not able to do any and everything that I used to.

I'm going to stock up on my favorite ice cream, get out to buy a martini when I can, and take it one day at a time. Oh, and I will also carry the twins to the library every weekend, so we can check out some of our favorite books, as well as some new ones to read. (By the way, I have submitted the proper paperwork to the Baltimore County Public Library for readers to check out my first book, and I hope that readers will be able to do so later this year.)

I hope you have enjoyed this book so far, and if so, take a break to have a martini with me, I call it a "Tam-tini." I prefer Ketel One, but grab your vodka of choice, and add the following, and enjoy!

§ Ketel One Vodka

§ Snapple (Orange Mango) juice

§ Garnish your glass with a fresh orange

FYI - My favorite martini is the Hawaiian martini from Bonefish Grill. It is beautiful and delicious. Please go and try one if you can.

PART III

POETRY

This next section of the book is dedicated to poetry. I like to write diverse types of poems to express how I'm feeling, to describe something I love, or just for fun.

These first three are about marriage and motherhood, my father, mother, and siblings.

Marriage & Motherhood

Nothing could've prepared me for these two choices.

No manual, no script, no perfect fit.

You go through the formalities, the rings, the place, the dress, the food—let's celebrate!

Then you get home and you better be able to talk, get along, you know communicate.

Be submissive they told me, a man needs to know he is "needed."

You've been taught to be strong and independent, but don't come off as too intimidating.

They say there will be some things you just have to accept because that's how men are.

But you are a woman and you feel like he's taking it too far.

You don't want to be challenged like this, because playing games can make you lose who you are.

Right away we start a family because that's what we both want to do.

But who can prepare you for a child or two.

Here they come, ready or not.

Pampers, bottles, sleepless nights it's a lot.

Maternity leave for me, back to work for him. You think it's going to be a breeze but it's not.

Year after year the struggle gets realer; and the reality of who we really are gets clearer.

Nobody ever said this would be easy.

Aiming to be a Good Wife and Good Mother.

Still trying to please be a good lover.

Now there's three people looking at me, depending on me.

Some days I'm so weary, I just want to BE…Me.

That's when I dig deep and pull from within.

Because I know that through it all I will WIN.

Nobody ever said this would be easy.

When I used to cry and think that I never could, the day came that I would embrace Motherhood.

When I cry and think about how we've both carried all this baggage, I know the day will come when we have a better marriage.

Nothing could've prepared me for Marriage and Motherhood, but thus far I have made it through all the bad and look forward to the good.

Tamara Harvey, 1/20/2018

Could've Should've Would've

Daddy, I wish you could've been mature and strong enough;

Loved us enough to want to stick around

Somebody should've been there to hold you accountable, as a father and a man

To tell you to do better for your family, you know the best that you can

We needed to learn something from you, not just have fun

You would've been proud of us, your wife, your daughter, your son

Nevertheless, I grew up and forgave you, formed a bond, because in life my father I'd only have one.

Coffee in the Morning

Mom, we kind of grew up together in a sense
You're just a few years older than me, almost like a sis

But you were my provider, guider, best friend, and advisor
With you I don't have to lie, and at most times, you are the only one I feel comfortable with to cry

Our endless phone conversations are never boring, and now that I'm older I look forward to them with coffee in the morning

A girl will have a lot of things in life, one after another, but there's only one that's irreplaceable and that's her mother

Big Sister

Being the oldest wasn't easy, it came with a lot of responsibility.

Help Mommy, help little brother, and baby brother too.

But as the Big Sister, who's going to help you?

I felt like a second mother, stepping up and taking charge.

When times were tough, I tried to be there no matter how small or large.

As we got older, things changed, and so did we.

But at the end of the day, some things will always remain the same.

We will always be each other's siblings, just us three.

PART IV

MY HAIKU

The rest of the book is a collection of my HAIKU poems. I like haiku poems because they are short and sweet. Even though they all may not have a "seasonal reference," I use the 5-7-5 format (five syllables in the first line, seven in the second, and five in the third).

What will quench my thirst?
I'll Have a Martini, Please!
Ketel One Vodka

Roses are pretty
That is my favorite flower
Red to be exact

Work, work, work, work, work
From sixteen to forty-eight
I want to retire

Rob Peter, pay Paul
Every two weeks the same thing
Try to stay ahead

Scorpio Woman
A mystery to so many
Loyal and loving to one

Who are you today?
This way or the other way
You're a Gemini

Yummy, I love it
Bananas, chocolate, and nuts
It's Chunky Monkey!

Your rhythm and pitch
It often takes me away
I Love You, music

Reading brings her joy
Imagining other thoughts
Then making them hers

Writing is all new
Doing it seems so easy
The right thing to do

Is it Lust or Love
That makes me do these dumb things
Still feeling lonely

You want to chit chat
Is that all you want from me?
Or, umm, more than that

My hair oh my hair
Some days a lot of concern
Others not so much

Just like a girlfriend
And always there to count on
I do love my wigs

Why can't I conceive
Is there a problem with me?
Wait on God and see

Church every Sunday
Bible study and worship
We need to go back

I am a Woman
And I am a Mother too
How Phenomenal!

Twins are a blessing
Yes, Jonathan and Janell
They are gifts from God

Fall is the best time
Days of brisk air darker nights
Perfect Thanksgiving

Let's go fly a kite
It sure is windy enough
The first day of spring

Hot just like summer
Comfortable in her skin
Waiting to be loved

Welcoming winter
Hot cocoa and cozy fires
Helps warm those cold nights

This world is scary
Too many unsafe places
Praying for world peace

Don't talk politics
Not in the office at least
Religion either

Arthritis is pain
Out of nowhere just hit me
Achy joints and knees

Aspercreme, BenGay
They do make me feel better
I don't like the smell

Lunch on a budget
Try quick and tasty pizza
From Little Caesars

Chinese for dinner
Where is my fortune cookie?
My lucky numbers

It starts as a drip
And then it just continues
Please fix the faucet

Cracked walls and old pipes
Oh, the house is settling
Endless home repairs

Sunlight shines so bright
Helping us get up and rise
A bright yellow star

I love a full moon
It's brightness and defined shape
Illuminated!

Winter, dark and cold
I don't mind though, I sleep more
Waiting for springtime

There's a pill for that
Oxy, Vikes, or Percocet
Opioid abuse!

Looking for a change
From the boring old cable
Well Hello Netflix!

My friend Alonza
He lets me sit on his couch
And we talk and talk

Oh, just fuck it all
The frustration and worry
Don't make things better

The best pleasure is
Orgasmic sex with my guy
Me, on top, control

She is not like me
Maybe that's why he likes her
And he is not him

Oh wait, now I see
You take 'blue pills' for ED
But not loving me

You know what they say
Once a cheater always one
Tell me about it

I guard it safely
Letting you in to love me
Please don't break my heart

I'll Have a Martini, Please!

To serve and protect
Making sure we are all safe
Thank you, Officer!

My favorite song
I hope you don't get "Famous"
By French Montana

Saturday morning
No school but still up early
Janell has art class

I ask, where are you?
Disconnected on FaceTime
Ha, technology!

I miss the old days
Sitting on Grandma's front porch
Laughing and joking

May you be happy
In whatever you desire
Good luck to you, friend

I need to have this
My coffee in the morning
It is my Me Time!

We used to hang out
Club hopping West Side East side
Then it got boring

Why are you confused?
One-minute men now women
Are you gay or not?

Hand on the Bible
I swear to tell the whole truth
Yes, I swear to God

Someone asked me this
Do hurt people hurt people?
Yes, absolutely.

Strive to be happy
Feel good about your own life
Not anyone else

Sweat under my breast
It's different, almost like a
Sour or a musk smell

That time of the month
Right before, I'm so horny
Just give me some love!

Explore your body
Look touch, smell, feel all over
Then you can show him!

Aquarius Man
Scorpio ideal partner
In bed, but not life

My Aquarians
I call them Thing 1 and 2
And I am the cat

Shopping for flat shoes
Is not easy for me y'all
Short girls want high heels

A Scorpio Scorned
Is a dangerous woman
No doubt she will sting

The silent treatment
Is necessary sometimes
Don't overdo it

A loveless marriage
Just makes it so hard to sleep
In the same bedroom

Sex, Drugs, Alcohol
Frequently go together
Just as good alone

People use *Money*
To control one another
But *it's* the Power!

How about Date Night?
You know just for me and you
We really need it!

Jerry, pick me up
I am no comedian
But I love coffee!

The house needs painting
But I can't climb the ladder
Too scared I might fall

Life is so draining
I'm grateful and so thankful
But I'm also tired

A cold Wednesday
Did not want to go to work
But the bills are due

Saturday morning
The local news, then Netflix
Now what's for breakfast?

Can't comfort you now
No, because I need it too
It's about me now

Saturday nights are
For watching Ms. Iyanla
Help fix people's lives

Mind, Body, Spirit
All need to be nurtured, and
Fed to be healthy

Ugh, I feel so bad
I told everybody No!
Like I should have done

HIV rate high
STDs, STIs too
Please BMore Careful!

Who is she?

Talkative when Comfortable
Always Giving the Benefit of the Doubt
Moody and Mean Sometimes
About Her Family
Ready to Receive Her Blessings
A Daughter, Sister, Wife, Mother, Friend

Acknowledgements

First and foremost, I want to give thanks to God, for every blessing he has given us, and for every one that is to come. To Jonathan and Janell, my love bugs; and my husband John for every memory we have shared over the last 10 years. I look forward too many more. As for my Goddaughter Morgan, I may not attend everything, but I will love you always. To my mother, Estella Jackson, you are the strongest woman I know. Thank you for believing in me and always talking and listening to me every day. To my brothers, James and Antuan, I love you both, and I wish you nothing but the best.

To my wonderfully supportive group of women I call my girlfriends, some of which are family; Lois Brinkley, Trenita Purdie, Angela Pompey, Shawn Bennett, Margot Blige-Holloway, Quandra Scott-Jones, Cynthia Keitt, and last but certainly not least Amelia Jones (my NY partner in crime). We have laughed, cried, worked, partied and celebrated many milestones together. I am truly grateful for our friendships.

Finally, to the Book Fuel team, everyone from each department for helping me along the way and again making my publishing dream come true.

References

Works Cited

Sorter, Toni. 2003. "Loneliness." In *Prayers & Promises for Women*, by Toni Sorter, 117. Uhrichsville: Barbour Books.

I Love Hate My Hair (My Journey with Alopecia) – is available to order from Amazon, Barnes and Noble, Apple iBook, Google Play, and Kobo books.

For more information about cancer, answers, hope, and to donate, contact the American Cancer Society at 1-800-227-2345 or visit their website at www.cancer.org.

Hertsch's Tavern aka "The Spot"

1902 Gwynn Oak Avenue

Gwynn Oak, Maryland 21207

(410) 944-6633

Visit my **It Works!** Website: **http://tamaraharveywraps.myitworks.com/**

Follow me on Social Media:

- Twitter - @Tscorp1111
- Facebook – TamNHarv
- Instagram - @tamnicharv OR @booksby-tamaraharvey
- Pinterest – tharvey8160
- Snapchat – tscorp1111

Email me at <ihamartinipls@gmail.com>

38125735R00080

Made in the USA
Middletown, DE
07 March 2019